DIY Shampoos to Restore Your Hair

Homemade Shampoo Recipes for Natural Hair

BY

Shawna S. Miller

Copyright 2020 Shawna S. Miller

License Notes

No part of this Book can be reproduced in any form or by any means including print, electronic, scanning or photocopying unless prior permission is granted by the author.

All ideas, suggestions and guidelines mentioned here are written for informative purposes. While the author has taken every possible step to ensure accuracy, all readers are advised to follow information at their own risk. The author cannot be held responsible for personal and/or commercial damages in case of misinterpreting and misunderstanding any part of this Book

Table of Contents

Introduction 5

1. Homemade Camphor Oil Shampoo 6

2. Mustard and Gray Clay DIY Shampoo 8

3. Honey Coconut Creamy Shampoo for Sensitive Scalp 10

4. 5-Ingredient Homemade Shampoo 12

5. Super Moisturizing African Black Soap Shampoo 14

6. Simple Oily Hair In-Check Shampoo 16

7. Sweet vanilla and Orange DIY Shampoo 18

8. Green Matcha Tea Hair Growth Shampoo 20

9. The Classic NO-Poo Shampoo 22

10. Apple Cider Vinegar-Castor Oil Shampoo 24

11. Homemade lemon Shampoo 26

12. Aloe Vera Essential Oil Shampoo for Strong Hair 28

13. Shampoo for delicate and soft scalp 30

14. Simple DIY Shampoo for Dry and Flaky Hair 32

15. DIY Dry Shampoo for Oil Hair 34

16. All Plant DIY Shampoo 36

17. Grapefruit Based Shampoo for Damage hair 38

18. Homemade Jojoba Shampoo for Dry and Brittle Hair 40

19. Simple Almond Oil Shampoo 42

20. No More Dry Scalp DIY Shampoo 44

21. DIY Egg Shampoo for Oily Hair 46

22. Apple Cider pH Balance Hair Shampoo 48

23. Thyme Lemongrass Shampoo 50

24. Lemongrass Dandruff Shampoo 52

25. Rosemary Herbal hair Shampoo 54

26. Beer to Bounce DIY Shampoo 56

27. Simple Dandruff Homemade Shampoo 58

28. DIY Re-Growth Shampoo 60

29. Argan-Based Soft and Silky Shampoo 62

30. Probiotic Moisturizer and Nourish Shampoo 64

Conclusion 66

Author's Afterthoughts 67

Introduction

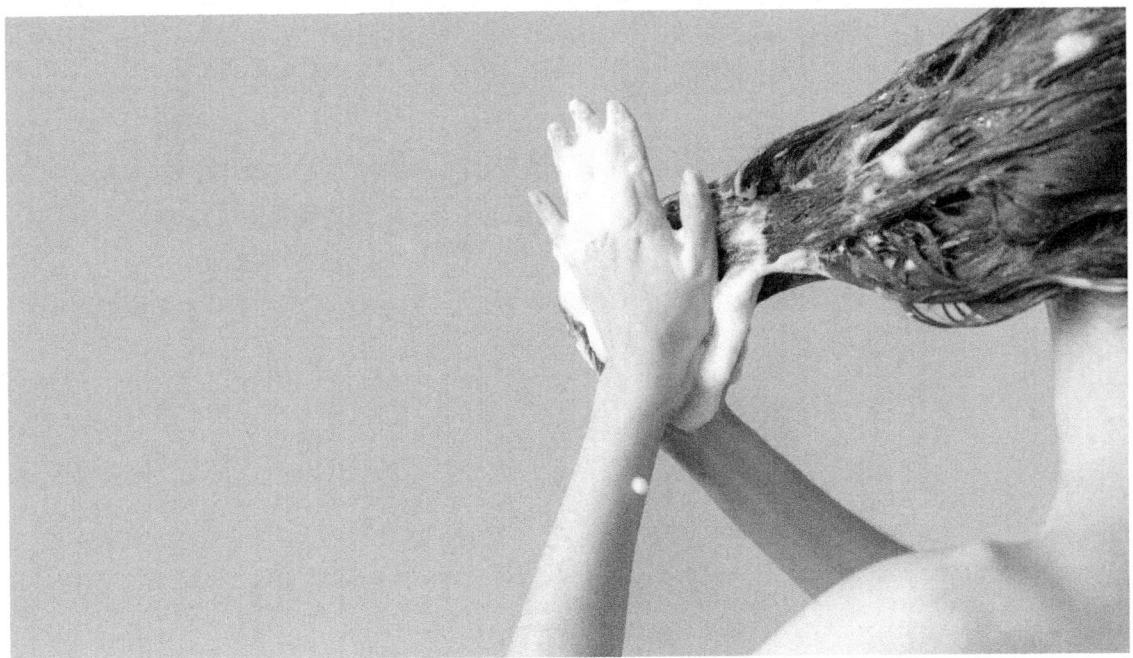

All we want is for our hair to look good, and it should not take that much to achieve it. Simple DIY shampoos are ingredients from your kitchen or local store that cater to the specific needs of your hair. Whether it is dry, oily, or curly, the following shampoos will change how you see your hair.

1. Homemade Camphor Oil Shampoo

Camphor has the same minty feel like peppermint. It stimulates the hair follicles, improves hair growth, and reduces fungus-causing dandruff.

For immediate use

Prep time 5 minutes

Ingredients

- 1 eggs yolk
- 1 tsp of camphor oil
- 1 tbsp Castile soap
- 2 tbsp distilled water

Method

Mix all the ingredients together

Ensure the oil is incorporated into the mixture

Apply and massage unto your scalp and hair

Allow it to sit for 5 minutes

Rinse off with lemon infused water

2. Mustard and Gray Clay DIY Shampoo

Although mustard is great for thickening hair, it has a potent drying powder and should be used scantily.

For one use

Prep time 10 minutes

Ingredients

- 1 tbsp gray clay
- 1 tbsp castile soap or shampoo base
- 1 tsp castor oil
- 1 tsp extra virgin olive oil
- 1 tsp mustard powder
- ¼ cup of water
- 5 drop of Ylang Ylang essential oil

Method

Mix the mustard powder and clay together in a bowl

Add the olive oil and castor oil; stir it well

Add the castile soap and use the water to loosen it

Fold in the drops of essential oil

Rub generously onto the hair, massage unto the scalp for 5 minutes

Rinse and condition

3. Honey Coconut Creamy Shampoo for Sensitive Scalp

Well, as said, shampoos don't have to have the lather to provide your hair with the desired nutrients.

For 1 use

Prep time 5 minutes

Ingredients

- ¼ cup of organic honey
- 1/8 cup fractionated coconut oil
- 3 drops of lavender oil (we choose this because lavender reduces scalp stress and triggers growth)

Method

Place the ingredients in a mix and whip it until fluffy

Scoop it into a container for use

To use, apply to each section and massage it unto the scalp

Rinse thoroughly and condition too

4. 5-Ingredient Homemade Shampoo

You do not have to have a barrage of ingredients to make your shampoo premium. Get the items that perfect for you and customize them to suit your needs.

Make 1 bottle

Prep time 10 minutes

Ingredients

- ½ cup of coconut milk
- 4 tbsp raw honey
- ½ cup shampoo base or castile soap
- 2 tbsp coconut oil
- 20 drops essential oil of choice

Method

Mix the castile soap and honey in a bowl

Add the milk and melted coconut oil

Pour into a pump-lid container and add essential of choice

5. Super Moisturizing African Black Soap Shampoo

This all-natural shampoo is all you need for all the hair problems you have. The combination of milk and essential oils provide the nutrients that your hair needs to keep it looking chic all day long.

Makes 1 liter

Prep time 1 hour

Ingredients

- ½ cup of coconut milk
- 1 tbsp honey
- ¾ cup grated original African black soap
- 1 tbsp coconut oil
- ½ tsp lavender
- ½ tsp tea tree oil
- ½ tsp castor oil
- ½ tsp almond oil
- 2 capsules Vitamin E

Method

Melt the African soap over low heat with the coconut milk

When it is fully melted, remove and stir continuously to mix well

Add the honey and coconut oil, still stirring it

As it cool, check the consistency, if it is too thick; add a little water to loosen it up

Add the essential oil and store in a container

It lasts for weeks.

6. Simple Oily Hair In-Check Shampoo

While oily hair is kind of nice, having too much makes your hair feel heavy and dirty. This shampoo will help you manage the excess oil without losing your sheen.

Prep time 5 minutes

Makes a small container

Ingredients

- ¼ cup castile soap
- ½ cup of coconut milk
- 20 drops almond essential oil
- 10 drops avocado essential oil
- 240ml distilled water

Method

Add the milk and water into the castile soap, mix well

Pour it into a squirt shampoo bottle

Add the essential oils and shake well

Use twice a week

7. Sweet vanilla and Orange DIY Shampoo

Give your hair the love and nutrition in this vanilla-based shampoo. It is easy, and your hair will thank you for it.

Makes for 1 use

Prep time 5 minutes

Ingredients

- ½ cup Castile soap
- 1 tsp vanilla oil
- 1 tsp honey
- 10 drops orange essential oil
- 5 drops of peppermint

Method

Add and mix the ingredients in a bowl

Pour into bottle

Apply on wet hair and massage well before use

8. Green Matcha Tea Hair Growth Shampoo

Stimulate the dermal papilla cells to improve hair growth and clean your hair with this shampoo.

Makes a bottle

Prep time 20 minutes

Ingredients

- 1 heap tbsp of green match tea brewed in 1 cup of water
- 1 tbsp raw honey
- 30ml castile soap
- 3 drops rose essential oil
- 5 drops tea tree oil

Method

Mix all the ingredients above except for the Matcha tea in a bowl

Ensure they are well mixed

Add the cold match tea while shaking to incorporate all ingredients

Use once

9. The Classic NO-Poo Shampoo

We have added a little more than the two ingredients to boost hair vitality and reduce scalp stress.

Makes a bottle

Prep time 10 minutes

Ingredients

- 1/3 cup shampoo base
- 1/3 cup water
- ½ tbsp baking soda
- 5 drops melaleuca oil
- ½ tbsp coconut oil
- 5 drops lavender oil

Method

Add the ingredients into the shampoo base container and shake

Remember to shake before each use too

Use once or twice, it will improve hair growth by reducing hair and scalp stress.

10. Apple Cider Vinegar-Castor Oil Shampoo

It works great to lose weight, and in your skin, ACV also does amazing things to your hair. It is paired with healthy fats to nourish your hair and strengthen it.

Makes 1 small bottle

Prep time 10 minutes

Ingredients

- 180ml coconut milk
- 1 tsp castor oil
- 1 tbsp honey
- 1 tsp apple cider vinegar – if you have oily hair, you can add extra
- ½ tsp Vitamin E
- 6 drops lavender oil
- 6 drop rosemary oil

Method

Add the honey, apple cider, and castor oil to the coconut milk

Mix well, and then add the specified drops of essential oil

Shake again and store for use

PS – you can use tea tree oil if you suffer from inflammation

11. Homemade lemon Shampoo

The lemon acts as a preservative, and it smells absolutely divine.

Makes a small container

Prep time 10 minutes

Ingredients

- 1 cup neutral unscented shampoo or ¾ cup castile soap
- 1 tbsp coconut oil
- 1 tbsp lemon juice
- 20 drops lemon essential oil

Method

Add the lemon juice and coconut oil to your base

Stir well until thick and pale

If it is too thick, add a little more coconut oil to loosen it

Add the essential oil and store

12. Aloe Vera Essential Oil Shampoo for Strong Hair

Do not let weak hair be a bother. This shampoo has all your favorite essential oil in one bottle.

Make 1 cup

Prep time 15 minutes

Ingredients

- ½ cup shampoo base liquid
- ½ cup aloe vera
- 5 drops of spearmint & chamomile essential oil
- 10 drops rosemary and lavender

Method

Whisk the essential oils with the aloe vera

Add it to the shampoo base and mix well

Pour into a squeezable container and use as desired

13. Shampoo for delicate and soft scalp

Sometimes regular shampoos are too concentrated for sensitive scalps. This is perfect for kids. Anyway, whether you are an adult or a child, this shampoo is refreshing and soothing on the scalp.

Makes 300ml

Prep time 10 minutes

Ingredients

- 10 drops citronella essential oil
- 10 drops tea tree oil
- 60ml castile soap
- 30ml coconut milk
- ½ cup distilled water

Method

Use the water to dilute the coconut milk

Whisk in the castile soap and then add in the essential oils

Pour into containers and use as desired

It is great for kids too.

14. Simple DIY Shampoo for Dry and Flaky Hair

Dry and flaky hair leaves your hair looking dull and unkempt. If you are looking for a shampoo to fix these problems, this shampoo is perfect for you.

Makes 2 cups

Prep time 15 minutes

Ingredients

- 40 drops – 10 each of lemongrass, rosemary, thyme, and lavender essential oil
- 15ml vitamin E (it allows it to keep for long)
- 30ml pure coconut oil
- ¼ cup manuka honey or raw organic honey
- 60ml coconut milk
- 120ml Castile base liquid soap

Method

Get a big shampoo container

Add all the ingredients in and shake it very well

Always shake before you and leave it on your hair for 5 minutes before rinsing out

15. DIY Dry Shampoo for Oil Hair

Yes, dry shampoo works well too!

Makes 1 small cup

Prep time 7 minutes

Ingredients

- 2 tbsp arrowroot powder
- 2 tbsp cocoa powder
- 5 drops peppermint essential oil

Method

Combine the powder in a bottle

Add the essential oil and shake it hard

To apply brush on the base and comb your hair

16. All Plant DIY Shampoo

It is easy to Make, but you have to keep an eye for the real Ingredients.

Makes about a liter

Time 60 minutes

Ingredients

- 12 pieces of Aritha or retha soap nuts
- 1 cup Amla gooseberries dried
- 6 pieces of Shikakai nuts
- 3 sprigs of rosemary

Method

Soak these four ingredients in 500ml of water overnight

By morning, add another 500ml and bring it to a boil for 5 minutes

It will be foamy, so please watch carefully

Allow the mixture to cool down and pour into the bottle

Use as desired and store any excess in the fridge

It is safe for pets too.

17. Grapefruit Based Shampoo for Damage hair

This shampoo uses infused grapefruit oil to stimulate hair follicles to improve hair growth and texture.

Make a small bottle

Prep time 10 minutes

Ingredients

- ½ cup of coconut milk
- 1 tbsp glycerin
- 1 tsp honey
- 1 tbsp grapefruit infused olive oil
- 5 drops grapefruit essential oil
- 3 drops lime essential oil

Method

Blend all ingredients in a blender except the essential oils

Pour into a container and add the essential oil

Use as desired

18. Homemade Jojoba Shampoo for Dry and Brittle Hair

This shampoo will lather just right to cleanse your hair and restore some life into it.

Makes a small bottle

Prep time 10 minutes

Ingredients

- 2 tbsp castile soap
- 2 tbsp vegetable glycerin
- 1 tsp jojoba oil
- A dash of argan oil
- 1 tsp coconut oil1
- ½ cup of water

Method

Mix all the ingredients together

Use immediately by massaging unto your scalp

Leave it to sit for 5 minutes before you rinse out.

19. Simple Almond Oil Shampoo

Almond contains all the vitamins that hair needs to heal and grow. In this recipe, we have combined three simple ingredients with some oils to repair your follicles and inflammation.

Makes 2 uses

Prep time 10 minutes

Ingredients

- ¼ cup mild Castile soap
- ½ cup goat milk (use coconut milk if goat milk is not available)
- ¼ cup of pure almond oil
- 10 drops tea tree essential oil

Method

Get a clean shampoo bottle

Pour the ingredients into it and seal

Shake with all your strength until it is incorporated

Always shake before use and rinse after

Massage the shampoo to the scalp

If you have inflammation, apply and allow it to sit for 10 minutes.

20. No More Dry Scalp DIY Shampoo

The biggest problem with growing natural hair is dryness. You can fix this problem by using this shampoo.

Make 2 uses

Prep time 10 minutes

Ingredients

- ½ cup cocoa butter melted
- ½ cup liquid castile soap
- 45ml wheat germ oil
- 45ml macadamia oil
- 30ml coconut oil
- 10 drops Ylang Ylang essential oil
- 10 drops Rose essential oil

Method

Whip the Castile base with the melted butter until fluffy

Add the oil and finally the essential oil

To use, massage a generous amount on your hair

Comb through and let it sit for 5 minutes

Rinse off and condition

21. DIY Egg Shampoo for Oily Hair

This is a one-use shampoo. Let's try it!

For 1 use

Prep time 10 minutes

Ingredients

- 1 large egg
- ½ tbsp Rhassoul clay
- 1 tbsp honey
- 1 tsp coconut oil
- 2 tbsp castile soap
- 2 tbsp water
- 10 drops of lavender and lemon essential oil

Method

Combine all the ingredients except the essential oils in a deep bowl

Using an emulsion blender, mix well and fold in the oils

Use in the shower

Please do not store

22. Apple Cider pH Balance Hair Shampoo

Apple Cider Vinegar is good at removing hair product residue from the hair. This shampoo uses a Castile base. You can omit it of your rather rub and rinse.

Makes for 1 use

Prep time 7 minutes

Ingredients

- 2 tsp Apple cider vinegar
- 1 Tbsp Castile soap
- 2 capsules of Vitamin E
- 1 tbsp coconut oil
- 5 drops jojoba oil
- 3 drops lemon verbena
- 1/3 cup of distilled water

Method

Add the apple cider to the water and pour it into the castile soap

Shake it very well; then add the coconut and jojoba oil

Give in another good shake

Add the essential oil and shampoo your hair

23. Thyme Lemongrass Shampoo

If you suffer from dandruff and hair loss, then we represent you to this shampoo. The combination in this recipe will enable you to manage both in one bottle.

Make 2 uses

Prep time 15 minutes

Ingredients

- 60ml castile soap liquid
- 1 cup thyme-infused distilled water
- 1 tsp avocado oil
- 5 drops lemongrass essential oil
- 1 tsp glycerin
- 10 drops lavender oil

Method

Mix the Castile and distilled water to combine

Add the glycerin and oil while whisking

Add the essential oils at the end

Always shake before you and rinse off properly

24. Lemongrass Dandruff Shampoo

This is the best homemade shampoo to solve your dandruff issue. With this shampoo, no more dandruff falling on your shoulders.

Make a bottle

Prep time 10 minutes

Ingredients

- 20 drops lemongrass oil
- 1 tsp glycerin
- 120ml distilled water
- 60ml castile soap
- 2 tbsp eucalyptus oil

Method

Blend everything together in a blender

Pour on a squeeze shampoo bottle

Use twice a week

25. Rosemary Herbal hair Shampoo

This recipe calls for herbal infused oil. We have infused fresh rosemary in raw tamanu oil for this recipe.

Makes 1 use

Prep time 15 minutes

Ingredients

- 2 ounces mild unscented castile soap
- 5 ounces rosemary-infused tamanu oil
- 5 drops lavender oil
- 5 drops clary sage oil
- 1 tsp of any preservative

Method

Whisk all ingredients in a bowl

Pour into a container

Always shake before use

Apply, massage, and leave on for 5 minutes

Massage some more and rinse off

26. Beer to Bounce DIY Shampoo

Bet you did not know that beer is good for hair too. It is loaded with proteins and vitamins that are great ingredients to restore the sheen and shine of your hair.

Make a bottle

Prep time 40 minutes

Ingredients

- 1 can of malt beer
- 1 cup of shampoo base
- 3 drops of lavender oil
- 2 drops of tea tree oil

Method

Bring the beer to a boil until it has reduced to a thick syrup

Allow it to cool down

Add it to the shampoo base and whisk properly

Mix in the essential oil

Pour into a container and use as desired.

27. Simple Dandruff Homemade Shampoo

The white flaky droppings can be embarrassing, but this shampoo will help.

Make 1 use

Prep time 10 minutes

Ingredients

- 1 tsp tea tree oil
- ½ tsp peppermint
- 5 drops of rosemary oil
- 3 tbsp coconut oil
- 1 tbsp raw honey

Method

If your hair is oily, this is not for you but if you suffer dry, itchy, and dandruff filled scalp, try it

Mix everything and apply unto the hair.

Remember to massage the scalp to remove any attached dandruff

Let it sit one for some minutes to enable the scalp to soak up the nutrients and eliminate as much of the flakiness

Rinse and condition, also apply a leave-in.

28. DIY Re-Growth Shampoo

If you suffer from hair loss, it can be hard getting the right shampoo. The ingredients in here will boost hair growth.

Makes 1 use

Prep time 15 minutes

Ingredients

- 60ml liquid Castile soap
- 60ml rice milk
- 3 drops lavender essential oil
- 1 tsp glycerin

Method

Whisk or use a hand emulsion blender to combine the ingredients

Wet the hair and apply generously from scalp to tip

Massage for 2 minutes, especially at the scalp

This opens the scalp and improves blood circulation

Rinse and condition

29. Argan-Based Soft and Silky Shampoo

Natural hair can feel dry and brittle sometimes. This homemade argan oil will add shine and texture for a smoother feel.

Makes a bottle

Prep time 20 minutes

Ingredients

- 120ml clean tap warm water
- 60m Castile liquid
- 15ml argan oil
- 7 drops jojoba oil
- 10 drops peppermint oil

Method

Whisk the ingredients together and pour it into an old shampoo bottle

Apply and massage through the hair

Rinse off and apply a second time

Wash and condition the hair

30. Probiotic Moisturizer and Nourish Shampoo

It is simple and totally organic for your natural hair.

Makes a bottle

Prep time 15 minutes

Ingredients

- 60ml unscented Castile soap liquid
- 1 tsp honey
- 1tbsp coffee
- 2 capsules probiotics
- 5ml vitamin E oil
- 60ml coconut milk
- ½ tsp olive oil
- 10 drops of rosemary oil

Method

Add all the ingredients into a blender and emulsify

Use as desired and store any remaining in the fridge

Do not allow water to get into the shampoo

It will breed bacteria and start to smell

Conclusion

Your hair can look as beautiful as you want without spending a whole lot of money or subjecting your hair to chemical damage. These 30 shampoo recipes are easy to make, they contain no preservatives hence cannot be kept for long.

Furthermore, remember to always condition your hair after every shampoo time; it helps remove any leftover residue. Enjoy!

Author's Afterthoughts

Thank you for reading my book. Your feedback is important to me. It would be greatly appreciated if you could please take a moment to REVIEW this book on Amazon so that we could make our next version better

Thanks!

Shawna S. Miller

Made in the USA
Middletown, DE
23 November 2020